Time Keepers

by Sita Sen   illustrated by Judy MacDonald

**Harcourt**

Orlando   Boston   Dallas   Chicago   San Diego

Visit *The Learning Site!*

www.harcourtschool.com

What Time Is It?

A long time ago people didn't think about time. People moved from place to place looking for food. They moved during the day when there was light. The day started when the sun came up and the day ended when the sun went down.

Then people started to stay in one place. They began to plant seeds and grow food. When to plant and when to harvest became a concern.

People watched the sun move in the sky. They watched the stars at night carefully, and they watched the moon. People tried to understand what they saw. They wanted to know more about day and night.

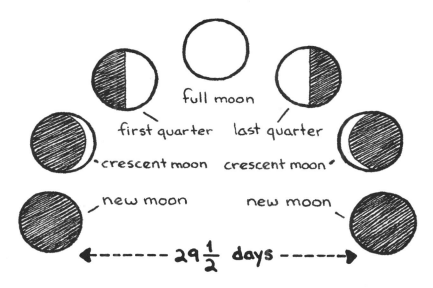

The Moon and Time

Many years ago people began to measure time by the moon. Changes in the moon are easy to see. At the time of the new moon, everything is dark. The moon cannot be seen. Every night, more of the moon can be seen. First, a crescent moon appears. Then, a quarter moon and then a full moon can be seen. After that, a quarter moon and a crescent moon can be seen. Then, the new moon starts again.

From one new moon to the next new moon is a cycle. From one full moon to the next full moon is a cycle. A cycle is a series of events. These events happen in a special order, and they happen over and over.

People paid attention to the cycles of the moon. It was easy to count the days in a cycle. A cycle of the moon lasts for about $29\frac{1}{2}$ days. Then the next cycle begins. It is easy to count cycles.

The early people named these cycles. Each cycle was a month. The word *month* comes from the word *moon*.

The Sun and Time

Long ago, some people did not mark time by the moon. The Egyptians, the Mayans, and other cultures had a different idea. They marked time by the sun.

They measured the length of the days by the sun's position in the sky. They noticed that the sun's position in the sky changed during hot and cold weather. They discovered that the sun is a better way to mark the year.

A Calendar and Time

Long ago, the Egyptians discovered that one star, the "Dog Star," came out next to the sun every 365 days. Near that same time, the water of the Nile River rose up and it covered the land nearby. The Egyptians used this information to make a sun calendar with 365 days. Today, most calendars follow the cycles of the sun.

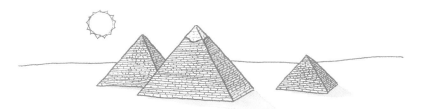

Longest Night

Longest Day

The Seasons and Time

Early people noticed something else as they watched the sky. On two days of the year, the hours of day and night are equal. These days come in the spring and in the fall.

People noticed that the longest day of the year was in the summer. The longest night of the year was in the winter. People used these two days to mark the seasons.

Early people discovered that each season lasted about three months. Each of these seasons had a cycle. Now people were able to measure a year.

The First Clocks

People continued to look for better ways to mark time. The early Egyptian people used shadows.

The Egyptians used obelisks to help them tell the time of day. An obelisk is a tall and narrow structure usually made of stone. The Egyptians noticed that obelisks made long and short shadows when the sun was out. These shadows moved as the sun moved.

The early Egyptians used the moving shadows to mark noon. The shortest noon shadow marked the shortest day of the year. The longest noon shadow marked the longest day of the year.

Then the Egyptians put stones around the obelisk to mark smaller parts of the day. When the sun was shining, obelisks helped the Egyptians divide their days.

The early Egyptians also used sundials. A sundial has a pointer which throws a shadow on a flat surface. The flat surface is marked with lines for each hour. The sun had to be shining for the early Egyptians to use sundials.

Some people tried water clocks. Water would drip from a high bowl to a lower bowl. The water dripped at the same speed all the time. The water would go up to a new mark on the lower bowl each hour.

More Clocks

Around 700 years ago, people started using new and different kinds of clocks. These clocks didn't need the sun, the moon, or water. These clocks were machines.

These clocks were placed in town squares so everyone could use them. Because they were so large, people could not have these clocks in their homes.

These big and heavy clocks did not work very well. They could not always tell the true time. They only had one hand and it pointed to the nearest quarter of an hour.

Finally, clocks were created that told the true time.

Clocks became fancier. Some clocks had bells that rang the hour. Some clocks had pictures on them. Some clocks had little birds inside that would come out to sing every hour.

As clocks got better, they got smaller. People began to carry watches. The first watches were kept in people's pockets. Then people started to wear watches on their wrists.

Paying Attention to Time

Today, everyone pays attention to time. Time has become very important. Cities and large towns have clocks outdoors. There are clocks in stores and in schools. Many people wear watches so they always know what time it is.

There are special watches for people who cannot see. These watches have strong hands which can be touched. These watches have raised dots instead of numbers. Today, some watches have calendars. Other watches have alarms.

What Time Is It?

A long time ago, people could not travel very far in one day. They could travel only as fast as a horse could go. When trains were invented, people could go hundreds of miles each day. Soon, trains could take people all over the country.

Time zones were created so people could know what time it was as they traveled. In the United States mainland there are four time zones: Pacific, Central, Mountain, and Eastern. Each zone represents a difference of one hour. When it is 12:00 noon Pacific time, it is 3:00 P.M. Eastern time.

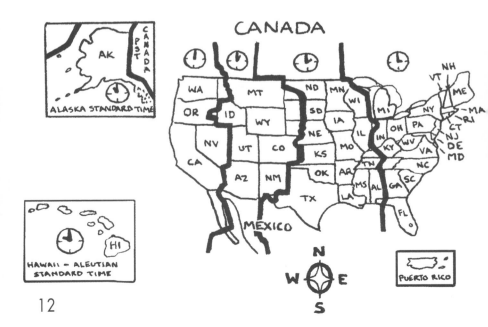

How Long Does It Take?

Today, some people time everything. How often have you heard the following phrases?

"How long does it take?"

"Do I have time for one more game?"

"What time is lunch?"

"How much time will it take to get there?"

When people travel, they are very concerned with time. They want to make sure they get to a place on time. People make plans based on how long a trip will take.

Someday people will travel to different parts of the universe. It will be important to know how much time people will need to travel.

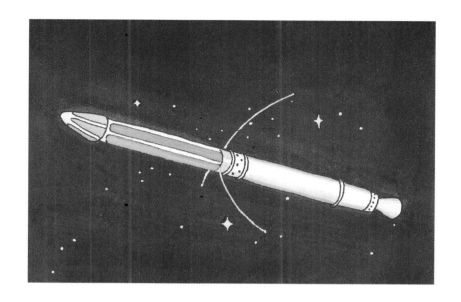

Time can be measured in minutes, hours, days, weeks, months, and years. Time can also be measured in very small units. A picosecond is the smallest unit of time scientists can measure. A picosecond is one-trillionth of a second!

Time can be measured in very large units, too. Scientists believe the universe is about 12 billion years old!

Time Talk

Here are some commonly used units of time:

A **minute** is sixty seconds.

An **hour** is sixty minutes.

A **day** is twenty-four hours.

A **week** is seven days.

A **year** is fifty-two weeks.

Ten years is a **decade**.